INNER * STRENGH

INNER STREENGTH

INTAL INTETER
STTRENGNTH
SNKΛW SRROVEL
AMVOVIVOTAT

INNER STRENGTH
ind notivatatione affirrations

TBREATKTHROWGH
THER ATHIVIC
BUCONCHMING
ONLLCOBTCLUNS
PERLEIVEIINIG
OPTTALK HROW
THE COBLOIVE
WALL
PS PRESEVEENICE

TTHERAPOVIC
MENTALL
THELL

OREAVKEK
THROUGH
WWALL

LSBA PRLZLS
AMERNOES!

neve tehblike

URTCERVECCE

PESNISIE

EVEHNG HIE
THERE IVES
GRACE

PESEVAVE
ARAUTTER PAWYW63T
- Ponere.

I AM
WORTHY
I AM STRONG

pORTTHY
I AM WORTHY

THEERAPIVICC
I AM WORTHY
only black outrrtny
BE AFSFRRLRSS. WRY

I AM
WORHTY

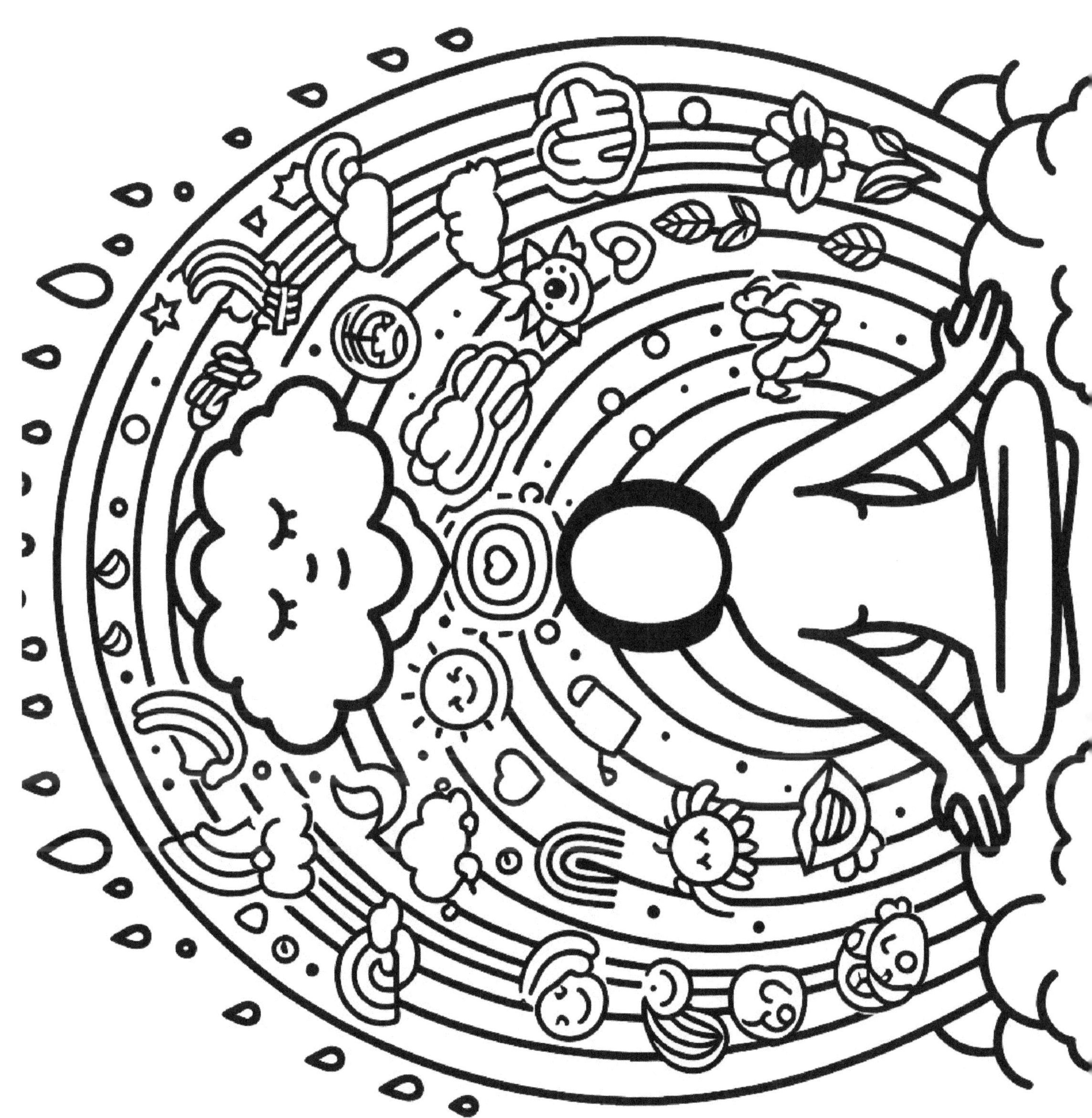

DREEAM CATCHERS

Inspoirring quotes about pursuing your dreams.

I AM WORTTY & STRONGY

I AM
I WORTHY
I AM
STRONG
THEAMPTIVE
AMEITHIATY

— I AM —
worthy
I AM STRONG.

CREATA
CELEBRATE
SMALL VICTORIES

CELLEBRATE
SMALL
VICTOIRIES

CELEBBRATE
MALL
VICTOIRIES

CELEBRATE
SMALL VICTORIES

Dream

THERAPIIC
MENITAL
color
your
your
dreams.